Workbook

For

Dr. Bessel van der Kolk's

The Body Keeps the Score:

Brain, Mind, and Body in the Healing of Trauma

Smart Reads

Note to readers:
This is an unofficial workbook for Dr. Bessel van der Kolk's "The Body Keeps the Score: Brain, Mind, and Body in the Healing of Trauma" designed to enrich your reading experience. The original book can be purchased on Amazon.

Download Your Free Gift

As a way to say "Thank You" for being a fan of our series, I've included a free gift for you:

Brain Health: How to Nurture and Nourish Your Brain For Top Performance

Go to www.smart-reads.com to get your FREE book.

The Smart Reads Team

Table of Contents

Overview of *The Body Keeps the Score*

The Body Keeps the Score, written by Dr. Bessel van der Kolk, is based on the simple premise that traumatic experiences – ranging from combat to childhood neglect, sexual abuse, and beyond – all have a lasting impact on one's brain and body. Published in 2014, the book covers a broad range of traumatic experiences and offers healing tools for both care providers and survivors of abuse. There is no such thing as 'light reading' for someone wanting to work through trauma. However, this book is easy to read, while taking a serious, in-depth look at facing—and overcoming—some painful topics.

Dr. Van der Kolk's work is backed by science that shows just how trauma changes the brain and nervous system. The text includes both personal examples of patients of Dr. Van der Kolk, as well as the results of relevant scientific research.

Dr. Van der Kolk discusses different types of abuse and explains three main avenues of healing. Many trauma survivors benefit from a combination of all three approaches, as there is no one avenue that works for all people. The text is designed to build a holistic understanding of trauma for healthcare professionals and abuse survivors alike.

Successfully explaining the history, impact, recovery, and context of traumatic experiences, *The Body Keeps the Score* offers insight into how the brain changes in response to trauma and provides a road map to navigate how to move beyond it.

Introduction

In the introduction to *The Body Keeps the Score,* Dr. Bessel van der Kolk emphasizes that trauma is a relatively common experience—perhaps more so than many realize. In his decades of work with trauma survivors, he has met victims of childhood physical and sexual abuse, those who bore witness to the abuse of others, veterans, and many others. He explains that trauma is often passed on to loved ones, meaning that the spouses, friends, and children of traumatized people are themselves often adversely affected by the mental injury.

For most people, the brain is not conditioned to move beyond trauma. Survivors find themselves plagued by nightmares, flashbacks, and physiological reactions to the trauma. However, new research across diverse disciplines is being pursued about improved ways to treat the effects of trauma.

Current research can generally be divided into three approaches to treating trauma: talking, forming meaningful human connections, and processing the memories of the trauma, which includes the use of medication to regulate the brain's response to triggering stimuli.

Van der Kolk cautions that there is no one-size-fits-all approach to treatment, and that most patients require a combination of treatment using the methods identified above.

The author's goal is to create a greater understanding of trauma as a way to empower others to explore how to best treat it.

Key Points

1. Overcoming trauma is not easy, but it is absolutely necessary for a positive, well-adjusted life.

2. Traditional talk therapy doesn't always work for people who have experienced trauma.

3. Dr. Van der Kolk believes that our bodies store trauma and cause physical ailments.

Part One: The Rediscovery of Trauma
Chapter One: Lessons from Vietnam Veterans

Summary

Dr. Van der Kolk begins by describing his work with his first patient, Tom, whom he met in 1978 while working as a psychiatrist at the Boston Veterans Administration Clinic. Tom was a successful lawyer, married with children, but was experiencing vivid nightmares of combat in Vietnam.

Dr. Van der Kolk prescribes pills to prevent the nightmares. Tom refuses to take them, stating that to do so would be to abandon his friends who had died in Vietnam.

Van der Kolk realizes that Tom's experience of trauma is more complex than he originally thought, and that medications alone are not successfully treating his nightmares.

Van der Kolk attempts to research Tom's condition, but finds very little medical literature on the subject. He reads *The Traumatic Neuroses of War* by Abram Kardiner, which suggests a physiological basis for post-traumatic stress. His only other sources of information are gleaned from observing his own patients.

Later, a patient named Bill is on the verge of being diagnosed by a different doctor with paranoid schizophrenia. He describes vivid flashbacks of dying children. After a Rorschach test reveals trauma, Dr. Van der Kolk realizes Bill is experiencing Post-Traumatic Stress Disorder (PTSD) as a result of his service in Vietnam.

The author emphasizes that, as most listeners react to accounts of trauma with horror, it is not surprising that the people who actually experienced the trauma are uncomfortable talking about it and, instead, try to forget it.

A talking cure, in which a survivor gains the ability to articulate what they have experienced, is rarely enough to heal the affected person.

The body itself needs to come to terms with trauma and recognize that the danger has passed.

Key Points

1. Trauma is more connected to our identities and physical senses than most people understand or realize.

2. Talk therapy alone is outdated for trauma treatment.

3. Prescription medications do not always work either, or patient cooperation can sometimes be a problem if the trauma causing the behavior is not addressed.

Questions to Guide the Reader

1. What was Tom's reaction to being prescribed medication, and why was Van der Kolk so surprised?

2. What did the Rorschach tests show during Bessel's nightmare study?

3. Why was Bessel so shocked when he changed jobs? What was similar and different between Harvard and the VA?

Chapter Two: Revolutions in Understanding Mind and Brain

Summary

Between his first and second years of medical school, Van der Kolk worked as an attendant at the Massachusetts Mental Health Center (MMHC). While there, he was able to observe patients to a degree that doctors could not. He speculates that the hallucinations patients often described may come from suppressed memories.

Van der Kolk also describes some violent methods of treatment he observed – notably, the force-feeding of a patient named Sylvia. Sylvia had been sexually abused by her brother and uncle. Holding her down for force-feeding replicated this trauma and caused further harm, which was counterproductive to her treatment.

As a psychiatrist, Van der Kolk developed an interest in neuroscience, believing it may lead to a greater understanding of trauma. He described the research of Steven Maier of the University of Colorado, in which Maier administered electric shocks to caged dogs.

When the doors of the cages containing the shocked dogs were opened, the dogs did not attempt to escape. The dogs who had not been shocked ran away immediately.

Van der Kolk drew a parallel between this behavior and the way some of his patients seemed to be psychologically "frozen" by their trauma.

The author also began to research the relationship between serotonin and PTSD. When Prozac was released in 1988, he began to prescribe it for his patients, often with successful results. However, while Prozac worked well for many trauma patients, Dr. Van der Kolk found that it had no effect on combat veterans.

Van der Kolk has no conclusive explanation for this observation, but rather uses it to demonstrate that pharmacology has its limits in treating trauma. In a frank critique of the American healthcare system, Van der Kolk asserts that drugs have become the default method of treatment because they are so profitable. He then states his intention to explore more holistic methods of treating trauma.

Key Points

1. Van der Kolk spent his short time at MMHC trying to understand the doctors' treatment of these patients, and the patients themselves, but there was no official recognition of certain disorders caused by trauma.

2. Van der Kolk recognized the insensitive and abusive treatment of these patients when he came up with a personal rule - question any practice or treatment that you wouldn't do to a family member or friend.

3. In 1980, the first Diagnostic and Statistical Manual of Mental Disorders (DSM) was published.

4. In 1988, Prozac was released, and Bessel began to study its effects on PTSD patients.

Questions to Guide the Reader

1. How did Dr. Van der Kolk's first job influence his later career working with trauma patients?

2. What did he learn about trauma after reviewing the "learned helplessness" trials that dogs went through?

3. The breakthrough of the DSM and the use of psychiatric drugs brought enormous changes to the psychiatric community. Discuss.

4. How and why are psychiatric drugs both good and bad for patients with psychiatric conditions?

Chapter Three: Looking into the Brain, a Neuroscience Revolution

Summary

In the 1990s, advancements in brain imaging technology led to an increase in neuroscience research. Van der Kolk used this new technology to conduct a study of brain activity during flashbacks.

He found increased activity in the limbic area of the brain, particularly the amygdala, which activates the body's response to stress.

He also observed decreased activity in the parts of the brain that process speech, leading him to conclude that there is a scientific basis for a patient's mental and physiological struggle to express their own trauma.

The brain scans also showed a shift in activity from the left side of the brain, most commonly associated with logic and analysis, to the right hemisphere, which is associated with emotion and creativity. The left side of the brain recalls the facts of an event, while the right side recalls how it felt.

In healthy people, the two sides of the brain work together in harmony. However, when one side is not functioning properly, it causes inappropriate reactions in social situations.

When the left side of the brain fails to function during the recall of trauma, the patient is unable to view the action analytically, in context, as an experience that happened a long time ago.

Although brain scans have been helpful in visualizing the effects of trauma, these images are still widely open to interpretation. Additionally, certain states of mind, such as denial, cannot be measured by brain scans. Researchers have found that scans are most effective at demonstrating when and how trauma is triggered.

Key Points

1. MRIs and PET scans finally showed doctors what was going on inside trauma patients' brains.

2. The left side (emotional side) of the brain lights up during flashbacks in trauma patients, but otherwise, shuts down.

3. After seeing these imaging results, Bessel's journey now becomes how to heal the left brain.

Questions to Guide the Reader

1. Which side of the brain is the rational side, and which is the emotional side?

2. How did MRIs and PET scans change the game of diagnosing and treating trauma patients?

3. How are trauma patients different from patients suffering from depression?

Action Plan: Part One

1. Identify the purpose of reading this book. If you are looking for answers for your own personal journey, consider this book with an open mind.

2. If you are living with your own trauma, this book should be considered informative only, and not diagnostic in any way.

3. Remember, the best way to address trauma and heal is to see a professional, who can help determine which of the therapies described in this book, if any, are right for you.

Part Two: This is Your Brain on Trauma

Chapter Four: Running for Your Life: The Anatomy of Survival

Summary

The chapter begins with Van der Kolk recounting his work with Noam, a child who was in school when the nearby World Trade Center was attacked on September 11, 2001. He, his teachers, and his schoolmates were able to escape safely. The following day, Noam drew a picture of the towers burning; however, he included a trampoline at the base of them to save anyone who chose to jump from the upper windows.

Van der Kolk immediately noticed that Noam's optimism in the wake of the attack stood in stark contrast to other trauma survivors. Many felt paralyzed in the wake of trauma, unable to move forward or plan ahead.

When a person feels trapped, the right side of the brain (or the emotional side) responds first to danger. When the brain is operating normally again, then the left brain is able to process and analyze the situation.

When the body is prevented from reacting, the balance between the two sides of the brain is destroyed, and the rational side of the brain is unable to perform its function.

Van der Kolk boldly states that "dissociation is the essence of trauma."

When traumatic experiences are shut down and not acknowledged, they frequently appear as flashbacks, nightmares, or panic attacks. They also result in increased production of stress hormones.

Brain scans show that, in terms of neurological activity, patients are unable to distinguish between past trauma and present danger. Van der Kolk asserts that it is not enough to desensitize patients to past trauma; they must learn "to live fully and securely in the present."

Key Points

1. There are three parts of the brain: reptilian, limbic, and rational.

2. Trauma affects all three parts of the brain.

3. How we learn to cope with stress as a child follows us into adulthood.

Questions to Guide the Reader

1. If a child learns to dissociate in response to stress, how might that person react to a car crash?

2. Which part of the brain develops first in children?

3. Which of the brain's parts does Bessel refer to as a "smoke detector" and which is the "watchtower"?

Chapter Five: Body-Brain Connections

Summary

In Chapter Five, Van der Kolk focuses on the research of Charles Darwin. Darwin asserted that humans and animals both express emotions the same way; thus, emotions serve a biological purpose for self-preservation.

However, when people are focused solely on survival, they show a reduced capacity for emotions.

Darwin also noted that strong emotions are felt physiologically as well as mentally. Contrary to others in the mental health field, Van der Kolk suggests that trauma survivors with substance dependencies are attempting to lessen the physical, rather than mental, effects of trauma.

The signifiers of emotion we observe in others are produced by the autonomic nervous system (ANS). In order to function correctly, the two branches of the ANS must function together in harmony. These are the sympathetic nervous system (SNS), which dictates our response to danger, and the parasympathetic nervous system (PNS), which deescalates our reactions. It also plays a role in healing wounds and digesting food.

Inhaling activates the SNS, while exhaling activates the PNS.

In 1994, researcher Stephen Porges used Darwin's observations to develop the Polyvagal theory, which argues that relationships with others are central to understanding and treating trauma.

One of the most damaging effects of trauma is the victims' real or perceived isolation from those around them. The ventral vagal complex of the brain, or VVC, allows members of a community to feel increased sympathy for one another through social interactions. This is vital to the healing process.

In trauma survivors, the VVC attempts to protect the victim by disengaging, even though this survival response is no longer required.

Van der Kolk states that one of the main aims of trauma treatment should be to reverse this process, allowing the patient to form meaningful connections with others again.

Key Points

1. The nervous system provides a body-brain connection.

2. Social support is the best way to protect ourselves from normal stress and trauma.

3. The three levels of safety are social engagement, fight or flight, and collapse.

Questions to Guide the Reader

1. How does the body react to trauma?

2. How many levels of safety do humans have?

3. How does rhythmic movement help trauma patients?

Chapter Six: Losing Your Body, Losing Yourself

Summary

Dr. Van der Kolk uses his personal experience with patients who have suffered abuse or neglect to assert that this type of trauma can damage one's sensory perception. The first story he recounts is that of a patient named Sherry, whom he sent to a massage therapist as part of her treatment to prevent self-harm.

Sherry later told Dr. Van der Kolk that she was unable to feel the sensation of the therapist's hands on her feet.

Other patients who had suffered similar abuse were unable to identify the approximate size and shape of objects placed in their hands.

Dr. Ruth Lanius, a fellow researcher, conducted numerous brain scans to analyze the patterns of the brain when subjects attempt to clear their minds. Studying both trauma patients and those who had not experienced trauma, Lanius observed that the ability of survivors to let their minds go blank was severely impacted.

Survivors demonstrated little self-awareness, and their ability to recognize changes in their own state was impaired.

Another researcher, Antonio Damasio, observed that traumatic flashbacks disrupt the body's regulation of basic functions. This can lead to inconsistent sleep or amnesia, overeating or little pleasure in eating, and anxiety. Van der

Kolk adds that he has observed that trauma victims often experience depersonalization, a feeling of disconnection from one's body.

Reestablishing an inner physical and emotional connection is a crucial early step in healing trauma.

Key Points

1. Trauma is manifested in the body as digestive problems, migraines, chronic pain, etc.

2. Once someone is traumatized, they tend to lose themselves after their brains shut down certain connections.

3. In order to regain full capacity, trauma patients must first learn to live in and feel their bodies again.

Questions to Guide the Reader

1. What is the body-brain connection?

2. How can trauma patients regain a sense of themselves after being traumatized?

3. Why is asthma more common in traumatized children than others?

Action Plan: Part Two

1. Practicing mindfulness can be a powerful tool in grounding patients back to their center and reconnecting to reality.

2. Practicing yoga can be a very efficient way for trauma patients to reconnect with their bodies.

3. Talking with trained professionals who know how to work with trauma patients is beneficial. Be sure to find a therapist who specializes in treating PTSD.

Part Three: The Minds of Children

Chapter Seven: Getting on the Same Wavelength: Attachment and Attunement

Summary

While working for the children's clinic in the Massachusetts Mental Health Center, Dr. Van der Kolk conducted an experiment in which he showed magazine cut-outs to the children and asked them to make up stories based on the images.

The children who had been abused told graphic and violent stories, even when shown neutral images. In one such example, Van der Kolk held up a picture of a man repairing a car, watched by two children. The story he received was that one of the children in the image beat the man to death with a hammer.

The children who had not been abused told positive, happy stories.

When parents raise infants, the children become accustomed to the patterns of their parents' movements and behavior. Children learn early social bonds through this type of attachment. Children who have been abused by their guardians have not experienced this attachment, instead learning from their experience of isolation.

Children who do not form appropriate bonds with their parents develop unhealthy coping mechanisms, which may range from isolating themselves to throwing tantrums for attention.

Children who have been traumatized by their parents may find themselves being unable to trust anyone, seeking intimacy from inappropriate sources, or even becoming physically immobile.

Children who show signs of what Van der Kolk calls "disorganized attachment" are substantially more likely to demonstrate self-destructive behavior as adults, such as substance abuse, promiscuity, and self-harm.

Van der Kolk states that he founded his Trauma Center in 1982 to develop programs that can correct the effects of disorganized attachment.

Key Points

1. Repeated trauma at an early age will develop into attachment disorders

2. Children who grow up in this environment turn into self-loathing adults

3. In order to heal from this sort of trauma, patients need to get back in touch with their bodies, to reconnect their bodies and brains.

Questions to Guide the Reader

1. Why is trauma so much worse if inflicted at a young age?

2. How can children develop insecure attachments, and what kinds are there?

3. How can victims of repeated trauma as a child begin to recover? What is the first step?

Chapter Eight: Trapped in Relationships: The Cost of Abuse and Neglect

Summary

Dr. Van der Kolk begins with his observations of his former patient, Marilyn, who, on the rare occasion that she entered into an intimate relationship, would begin physically abusing her partner. She had no understanding of what caused these violent outbreaks and told Van der Kolk that she often felt numb. Additionally, she demonstrated physical symptoms such as rapidly deteriorating eyesight and bouts of vertigo. Marilyn was eventually diagnosed with an autoimmune disease called lupus erythematosus.

She seemed to have little recollection of her upbringing. This, in tandem with her other symptoms, led Van der Kolk to believe she was demonstrating psychological symptoms of surviving incest.

Marilyn was Van der Kolk's third patient that year who was diagnosed with an autoimmune disease after a suspected history of incest.

Marilyn only began to open up about her childhood abuse when a fellow patient in her therapy group shared the story of her own childhood sexual assault. Her memories returned out of order, many in the form of dreams, and were extremely painful to recall. Her healing was aided by what Van der Kolk calls "the life force," or the will to live.

Key Points

1. Children develop insecure attachments when their caregivers are the cause of their trauma.

2. As adults, especially female survivors of incest, they will likely develop physical manifestations of their trauma, such as autoimmune disorders.

3. The rational brain cannot override the emotional brain if the emotional road map of decision-making is askew.

4. Trust issues are at the root of many problems these adults have in their lives.

Questions to Guide the Reader

1. Why are victims of incest more likely to develop autoimmune disorders as adults?

2. How does a child "deal" with living with their abusers?

3. Give an example of how manifestations of distrust can develop as these victims age.

Chapter Nine: What's Love Got to Do with It?

Summary

Van der Kolk states that trauma patients seeking treatment sometimes receive as many as five or six diagnoses or medication prescriptions over the course of their recovery. He emphasizes that these diagnoses are rarely wrong, per se, but all fail of them to address the root cause of the issue.

Mental illnesses are too complex to be labeled by a simple blanket term, such as "Major Depressive Disorder" (MDD).

Receiving a psychiatric diagnosis may have serious ramifications for a patient, but diagnostic processes vary widely among prescribers. Psychiatrists also frequently diagnose patients based on surface issues that mask the root issue. Substance abuse, self-harm, and eating disorders are often rooted in childhood trauma, but treatments are prescribed based on a single action.

Van der Kolk observed that the main determining factor in whether an adult coped with stress through healthy or harmful methods is whether they experienced childhood abuse.

Key Points

1. The author studies borderline personality disorder (BPD) patients and finds an obvious link between that diagnosis and childhood abuse, which propels

him to propose splitting PTSD into that and a subcategory of complex post-traumatic stress disorder (CPTSD).

2. Further research at an obesity clinic finds that many common problems have obvious links to childhood abuse: alcoholism, substance abuse, self-harm, BPD, obesity, the risk of participating in unsafe behaviors, etc.

3. The Adverse Childhood Experiences or ACE study finds that the higher the ACE score is, the more likely someone is to participate in these risky behaviors or have these problems later in life, on an exponential scale.

Questions to Guide the Reader

1. What is the difference between PTSD patients who have recent trauma or have recently survived a natural disaster, and the PTSD patients who are suffering from childhood abuse (as adults)?

2. What is the Traumatic Antecedents Questionnaire or TAQ, and why was it important in the development of taking trauma histories?

3. What did the ACE study's first round of interviews prove about child abuse?

Chapter Ten: Developmental Trauma: The Hidden Epidemic

Summary

Dr. Van der Kolk begins chapter ten with the case studies of three traumatized children: Anthony, Maria, and Virginia. All three were diagnosed with a range of mental illnesses, including depression, anxiety, ADHD, and PTSD. None of the diagnoses addressed what was actually "wrong" with the children. The most common explanation the children were told was they simply suffered from "bad genes."

Van der Kolk explains that this is not true in the way medical professionals once thought.

> **Parents do not transfer undesirable mental traits to their children. The change is epigenetic, meaning that the body's response to danger is permanently changed.**

Van der Kolk goes on to explain that developmental disruption begins with childhood trauma, which affects the patient's ability to socialize in a healthy manner preceding and during adolescence. This particularly affects their ability to develop and maintain relationships after puberty.

The fifth edition of the American Psychiatric Association's Diagnostic and Statistical Manual of Mental Disorders (DSM-V) does not include what Van der Kolk calls "Developmental Trauma Disorder."

This failure to address the effects of childhood trauma correlates directly with the United States' incarceration rates.

Van der Kolk points out that, in recent years, countries in Western Europe have spent more money on diagnosis and treatment of childhood trauma, but much less on prisons, which has already shown a decrease in their national incarceration rates.

Key Points

1. In 2009, Bessel submitted a proposal for a new diagnosis for these children: Developmental Trauma Disorder.

2. The DSM-III defines PTSD as a person who has witnessed a horrific event, which affects their interpersonal relationships, intrusive "reliving" of the event, and sometimes involves amnesia.

3. DSM-V comes out, and has hundreds of new diagnoses, making the accurate ones less valid.

4. The research shows, again and again across the developed world, that social support for children is necessary for healthy development.

Questions to Guide the Reader

1. How has the DSM changed since its first publication, and how has it improved? At what point did the DSM begin to restrict diagnoses and treatment, and why?

2. Why did the NIMH denounce the DSM-V?

3. What happens when countries invest in healthy children? How are crime rates and incarceration affected and why?

Action Plan: Part Three

1. Parents can learn here that their relationships with their children (or future children) *will* affect their kids for the rest of their lives - including unexpected potential dangers of inappropriate attachment.

2. Those who are searching for answers and believe there is a root from a dicey family history may use this narrative as instructive, but again, never diagnostically.

3. Remember, the best way to proceed, if trauma is a potential issue in your life, is to see a professional who specializes in trauma treatment.

Part Four: The Imprint of Trauma
Chapter Eleven: Walk Slowly, But Never Backward

Summary

Chapter eleven begins with a case study of Julian, a member of the United States Air Force who experienced childhood sexual trauma at the hands of Catholic priest Father Paul Shanley. Julian, who had repressed this trauma until adulthood, came forward after his girlfriend made him aware of an article in the *Boston Globe* reporting that Shanley had been accused of child molestation.

As with Van der Kolk's previous patient, Marilyn, Julian's memories returned in fragments and out of order.

Van der Kolk cites the research of Pierre Janet, a nineteenth-century psychiatrist who established the terminology "narrative memory" to describe a victim's compulsion to reenact or exaggerate a traumatic memory. Janet is widely credited as being the first to use the term "dissociation" to describe the way in which patients compartmentalize their trauma.

Other early psychologists, notably Sigmund Freud, are credited with developing the "talking cure," one of the most common therapies available to victims today. However, many patients do not process their trauma through speech, but through reenactment, as with those observed by Janet. Van der Kolk cites this as the reason the actions of trauma survivors are frequently misinterpreted.

Key Points

1. Ever since the nineteenth century, doctors of mental health issues have seen and recorded PTSD.

2. Today, the "talking cure" (cognitive behavioral therapy or CBT) remains the most widespread treatment for PTSD.

3. As long as PTSD is not recognized and patients are continuously labeled "bipolar" or "oppositional" and no histories of the patient are taken into account, they will continue to fill our prisons and welfare systems.

Questions to Guide the Reader

1. How was Irene affected by her mother's death?

2. When was the word "dissociation" coined and does it still mean the same thing today?

3. Why are some memories "repressed" and why are some regular memories?

Chapter Twelve: The Unbearable Heaviness of Remembering

Summary

At the end of the Victorian era, interest in psychology began to diminish. It increased again during World War I, when those returning from combat demonstrated psychological symptoms that had not been previously observed.

A new diagnosis, termed "shell shock," was coined, but it was immediately forbidden by the military from being used in hospitals and medical reports, as Allied forces feared that the term would cause panic and uncertainty. The term continued to be used throughout World War II and into the early 1960s, as psychiatrists observed a pattern of dissociation common among combat veterans.

This same pattern is also observed in other trauma patients.

Van der Kolk shares the story of his patient, Nancy, who experienced trauma after being given insufficient anesthesia during an operation, then forced to remain awake for its duration. As in other cases Van der Kolk had observed, her recollection of the event initially came back in dreams, then in flashbacks.

Nancy was only able to begin healing when she began practicing Pilates. The increased strength in her physical core, improved self-awareness, as well as the new support community she built in her athletic classes, helped her leave her trauma in the past and begin to move forward.

Key Points

1. After Freud's death, the subject of trauma was no longer of interest to the general public; therefore, it was not researched as frequently.

2. In the 1990s, False Memory Syndrome was being used to explain traumatic incidents and prove other (true) accounts to be viewed skeptically or as untrue.

3. Remembering regular, but still intense and important, events is not like remembering traumatic ones.

Questions to Guide the Reader

1. How did Nancy finally recover from her traumatic surgical experience?

2. Why are traumatic memories so different from regular ones? In which ways are they most different?

3. What is False Memory Syndrome?

Action Plan: Part Four

1. For those who have experienced trauma, having flashbacks of memories and acting oddly are actually common effects seen in most trauma patients.

2. Working with a professional can help the patient feel more confident and grounded in reality.

3. A classic hallmark of a memory that has traumatic components is the way the memory comes to the surface: does it float up in a narrative way, with a beginning, middle, and end? Or is it murky and primarily sensory? Knowing what you remember is just as important as knowing why you remember something in a particular way.

Part Five: Paths to Recovery
Chapter Thirteen: Healing from Trauma: Owning Yourself

Summary

In order to recover from trauma, which leads many to feel as though they no longer possess ownership of their minds and bodies, that sense of ownership must be reestablished. According to Dr. Van der Kolk, there are four principle ways to achieve this: becoming calm and focused, maintaining calmness during triggering events or statements, living in the present, and not needing to keep secrets from oneself or others.

Van der Kolk examines several techniques for controlling one's physiological response to stimulation.

The regular practice of yoga has been shown to help patients remain relaxed even when experiencing flashbacks. Mindfulness techniques allow patients to experience how emotion affects physicality and vice versa.

All patients require different forms and applications of therapy, but Van der Kolk emphasizes that the goal is always to retrain the patient's mind to process the trauma as an ordinary memory, rather than as a clear and present danger.

Van der Kolk also emphasizes that this end is more important than the means, which may include treatments such as medication or Cognitive Behavioral Therapy (CBT). Bill, the patient mentioned in the first chapter, still suffers from flashbacks, but has found that Bikram yoga prevents him from feeling overwhelmed when they occur.

Key Points

1. In order to heal, the trauma must be confronted, but in a safe way - mindfulness, rhythmic movements, deep breathing, yoga, etc.

2. Prescription drugs can be effective, but they also have many downsides, including the potential for misuse or addiction and the further isolation that comes with the numbness of certain drugs (benzos and antipsychotics, especially). These should be prescribed with great care, and never enough at one time for a patient to abuse.

3. CBT is effective for most people seeking talk therapy, but desensitization to triggers with PTSD patients are super tricky and will often come with other negative emotions.

4. If individuals struggle to connect with other people when navigating these episodes and during their progressive recovery, they may be able to connect with an animal, like a dog or a horse.

Questions to Guide the Reader

1. How does dancing or martial arts help us reconnect with our bodies?

2. When all else fails, which of these would be most helpful to a trauma survivor: a therapist with a "go

getter" attitude, group therapy, or a group yoga and mindfulness class?

3. How is treating a patient with PTSD from a car accident different from treating a patient with PTSD from incest or physical child abuse from caregivers?

4. Treatments for PTSD patients often only include drugs. How can these treatments be expanded to make them safer and more effective than drugs alone?

Chapter Fourteen: Language: Miracle and Tyranny

Summary

In a survey, 225 survivors of the attack on the World Trade Center identified the following therapies as the most helpful in processing their trauma: acupuncture, massage, and yoga. Notably absent is the traditional "talking cure," prompting Van der Kolk to dig deeper into the positive and negative ramifications of talking about personal trauma.

Due to the way trauma disrupts our language, traumatic events are extremely difficult to describe.

Talking about trauma is one way to acknowledge what happened, and acknowledgment of the event is a necessary step in gaining power over the trauma itself.

Van der Kolk references Helen Keller's mastery of communication as a "birth into selfhood," a tool which allowed her to feel like a part of the world around her despite her physical limitations.

Van der Kolk goes so far as to state that "communicating fully is the opposite of being traumatized."

However, language presents various limitations in overcoming trauma. Many are uncomfortable hearing secondhand accounts of trauma. This serves to further reduce the community of support necessary to overcome the stigma of abuse and reinforce acceptance by others. Additionally, many trauma survivors find that they become genuinely speechless due to trauma's stranglehold on the parts of the brain that control language.

Even when not addressing their trauma, survivors have been observed to have more difficulty verbalizing than those who have not been traumatized. Dr. Alexander McFarlane conducted an experiment in which he asked subjects to name as many words beginning with the letter "b" as they could in sixty seconds. For participants who had not experienced trauma, the average number was fifteen. For PTSD survivors, the average was between three and four words.

Van der Kolk also cautions that focusing too much on language shifts patient care from compassion to a cold and impersonal clinical rationale. He maintains that the goal of a therapist should always be to support the patient in restoring their mental and physical well-being, not by causing them to conform to any perceived social conventions.

Key Points

1. CBT is effective for most people seeking talk therapy, but desensitization to triggers with PTSD patients are super tricky and will often come with other negative emotions. Therapists also often use appeals to the rational brain to "retrain" the emotional brain, which simply does not work.

2. The biggest mistake some survivors face is staying silent, which causes them to be at constant war with themselves. Using so much energy to fight a struggle within themselves causes people to shut down.

3. Self-awareness brings healing to survivors, because it leads to connections with other people, and, ultimately, full connection within themselves.

Questions to Guide the Reader

1. As we've seen throughout this book, natural treatments tend to be more effective. List some treatments that do not require prescription drugs or traditional talk therapy.

2. How can reconnecting with themselves help survivors move past trauma?

3. How can writing a letter to yourself help you discover hidden pains and memories?

4. What is a "top-down" approach in therapy, and why does it not work for PTSD survivors?

Chapter Fifteen: Letting Go of the Past: EMDR

Summary

Dr. Van der Kolk begins chapter fifteen with the case study of David, now a middle-aged patient who was assaulted in his early twenties, causing him to lose an eye. Dr. Van der Kolk attempted to observe the efficacy of a treatment method known as Eye Movement Desensitization and Reprocessing (EMDR). After asking David to recall the attack, Dr. Van der Kolk asked him to follow the movement of his index finger with his functional eye.

The doctor then repeated the process with other traumatic events in David's life. By the end of the session, the patient seemed calmer, and his eye showed increased function. The rapid eye movement allowed David to consign his painful memories firmly to the past, thus preventing him from having present physiological responses to the trauma.

David found that continued therapy allowed him to rebuild relationships with loved ones and find enjoyment in new hobbies.

EMDR was initially discovered by psychologist Francine Shapiro, who observed that she felt relief from her own traumatic memories when experiencing rapid eye movement. When Van der Kolk tried it himself, he found it worked so well that he began incorporating it into his regular practice, finding it particularly effective for patients who did not speak English.

How exactly EMDR works is not yet understood, although it is believed that the technique brings traumatic memories to the surface and allows them to be newly associated with other memories.

Van der Kolk states that a psychiatrist's duty is to treat the patient effectively, even if they do not fully understand how or why some exercises work.

Key Points

1. EMDR works by allowing the patient to integrate traumatic memories and separate them into a "that was then, this is now" context.

2. EMDR has been shown to have lasting effects, even after only one or two sessions.

3. This technique tends to be more helpful with those who were traumatized as adults, but it does still have a small success rate (completely cured of PTSD symptoms) with people abused as children. However, since childhood attacks change brains in their formative years, they are much more complicated to treat.

4. There is a correlation between the success of EMDR and the rejuvenation related to REM sleep, which can also be significantly disturbed by PTSD.

Questions to Guide the Reader

1. What is EMDR and how does it work?

2. How can EMDR help patients of PTSD in particular?

3. How is EMDR related to sleep?

Chapter Sixteen: Learning to Inhabit Your Body: Yoga

Summary

The author tells of a patient named Annie, who, upon her first visit to him, was too scared to speak. Rather than forcing conversation, he utilized qigong, a system of coordinated movement and meditation, which was taught to him from a Chinese student.

After asking Annie to observe how her body felt during the exercises, he soon discovered that she was a survivor of childhood abuse at the hands of her parents. For the first two years of her healing, her therapy was primarily physical as she continued to be uncomfortable discussing her abuse.

In 1998, Van der Kolk's trauma center began offering yoga as a form of treatment. Additionally, Van der Kolk was able to observe heart rate variability (HRV), which indicated whether a patient was in control of their present feelings.

Trauma survivsssssors who are not in control of their emotions have a slower heart rate and shallow breathing. The Trauma Center used hatha yoga to improve patients' breathing, which led to a decrease in their HRV.

As yoga promotes mindfulness, patients became more self-aware in other ways, stating that yoga helps them to recognize triggers more easily and improves their ability to make decisions.

Annie later told Van der Kolk that she still sometimes experiences flashbacks, but that she has learned how to keep her feelings from overwhelming her. Her continued practice of yoga also facilitates her ability to be more open with others.

Key Points

1. HRV measures how well the sympathetic and parasympathetic nervous systems work together - a general way to measure good health.

2. Yoga naturally lowers the HRV.

3. Yoga helps patients recover autonomy over their bodies and be comfortable in their own bodies again.

Questions to Guide the Reader

1. What is HRV and why is it an important metric for measuring a PTSD patient's recovery?

2. How does yoga lower HRV?

3. How can yoga help a sexual assault survivor learn to feel their body again?

Chapter Seventeen: Putting the Pieces Together: Self Leadership

Summary

A woman named Mary was Dr. Van der Kolk's first experience with a patient battling Dissociative Identity Disorder (DID). On an unscheduled visit to his office, she introduced herself as an oddly dressed woman named Jane, who claimed that Mary had been telling lies about her. As the session continued, two other personalities, a child and a teenage boy, made appearances.

Dissociation is very common in traumatized people, and the "splitting" of identities is simply one type of dissociation.

Dissociation develops as a survival strategy to prevent further pain to oneself. Though for many this is a temporary escape, for some traumatized people, this becomes a long-term coping mechanism.

Van der Kolk observes that everyone's personality is made up of various parts, any of which can become dominant in a given situation. Trauma, however, disrupts normal brain function and encourages survivors to view all of their personality components as separate and independent identities.

Van der Kolk cites another patient, Joan, who, after experiencing abuse as a child, believed she was unable to determine which of her identities was the real her. Asking her to validate the different aspects of herself without ranking any of them over the other, Van der Kolk was able to help her accept that conflicting feelings and thoughts, all within the same person, are entirely normal.

Dr. Van der Kolk offers the solution to this type of dissociation as self-leadership, which places the onus on the patient to understand themselves and their personality.

Key Points

1. DID can occur in extreme situations when a patient subconsciously "breaks off" into distinct personalities.

2. In order to be a whole person, the abuse survivor must regain control and "leadership" of themselves.

3. By acknowledging not only the trauma, but their current circumstances, patients can find a new way to live, and be in charge of themselves.

Questions to Guide the Reader

1. Why is DID so polarizing?

2. How does DID develop?

3. Why must someone be "in charge of themselves" in the first place?

Chapter Eighteen: Filling in the Holes: Creating Structures

Summary

Many trauma patients who have made progress with some forms of treatment have found that they still feel a "void" or emotional hole due to their past experiences. Van der Kolk emphasizes that it is one thing to acknowledge the trauma and develop healthy coping mechanisms, but overriding that feeling of emptiness is another.

Author Albert Pesso is credited as the progenitor of a technique that requires patients to create a "tableau" or dramatic depiction of their trauma. In this method, the patient takes on the role of the lead in a play and directs loved ones or group therapy members to reenact the event. Van der Kolk has stated that he is continually impressed by his patients' precision when they direct using this technique. Trauma survivors who benefit from drama therapy often know exactly where and how they want their "players" to behave.

Van der Kolk also has found that allowing the patient to cast another person as a central figure in their past has been particularly effective in this type of therapy. This method allows patients both to share their truth as well as reenact the story with a positive ending instead of the trauma they suffered.

Key Points

1. Directing a play of one's own life can be extraordinarily therapeutic.

2. The creation of a graphic representation or "tableau" allows patients to "redirect" their lives.

3. Patients can also fill in gaps in memory, or even "recast" important people from their past, to help let go of the trauma and its impact on their lives.

Questions to Guide the Reader

1. What is a tableau?

2. How does directing a play about yourself help access and assuage trauma?

3. Why is it important that the patient be the protagonist and the director of their play?

Chapter Nineteen: Rewiring the Brain: Neurofeedback

Summary

Different types of mental activities result in different patterns within brain waves, which can be observed via electroencephalogram or EEG. A study from 2000 shows that traumatized subjects demonstrate abnormal EEG readings even when observing images unrelated to their trauma.

Brain scans from trauma patients often don't demonstrate any patterns at all, prompting Dr. Van der Kolk to search for a way to restructure these abnormal EEG results. The result was a technique called neurofeedback.

Neurofeedback uses neural sensors to force the brain to produce more of certain frequencies and less of others. This "tricks" the brain into creating healthy patterns, which it is then able to replicate on its own.

Neurofeedback is a form of conditioning that can be used to reward desirable responses and discourage undesirable ones. Its use has primarily been to enhance performance in athletes and musicians, although recently it has been tested as a technique to treat ADHD.

At present, the technique is still new, and it has not been used to treat trauma in any significant capacity. However, Van der Kolk has begun experimenting with neurofeedback as a potential treatment for substance abuse and developmental trauma. Initial feedback from patients suggests that it may decrease anxiety.

Key Points

1. Neurofeedback is a way to rewire the brain, literally. It is a technique that changes the way the brain rewards and punishes certain mental criteria.

2. This technique is used mostly at this time for performance enhancement, but there is a logical connection between neurofeedback and potential treatment of trauma.

3. Scientists have begun experimenting with this as a treatment for ADHD, with promising results.

Questions to Guide the Reader

1. What is neurofeedback?

2. Why does Van der Kolk feel as though watching brain scans is comparable to having a conversation?

3. What is the most prevalent use of neurofeedback right now?

Chapter Twenty: Finding Your Voice: Communal Rhythms and Theater

Summary

Dr. Van der Kolk recalls his son's experience with chronic fatigue syndrome. At first, the affliction affected his ability to participate in various activities. After joining an improvisational theater class, however, he started playing powerful, confident roles. This led to a decrease in his chronic fatigue, which eventually disappeared altogether.

This is not the first time Van der Kolk has seen the positive effects of theater, which he finds particularly useful in enabling combat veterans to cope with PTSD.

He even speculates that Greek tragedy may originally have been a form of "ritual reintegration" for those who had served in the military (which, in ancient Athens, meant all male citizens).

Van der Kolk discusses the role of music in the civil rights movement and the South African Truth and Reconciliation Commission, and in raising soldier morale during warfare.

Theater has several advantages in the treatment of trauma. For one thing, many of the greatest dramas are about traumatic circumstances and have a cathartic effect. The act of staging a play also allows for less self-conscious engagement in a group with a shared objective, an activity in which each participant is essential.

The author relays the story of a girl who continually ran away from foster homes. She began participating in a

Shakespearean program that was staging a production of Hamlet, in which she was playing Ophelia. Despite her intense nervousness, she did not run away from the program, because she felt a sense of obligation to the group, as the play could not proceed without her.

Other participants in theater programs talked of the satisfaction of creating something powerful and being more "in the world" than they had previously thought possible.

Key Points

1. Drama therapy has a proven, valuable role in the treatment of trauma.

2. Many participants feel as though they can step into another's shoes or feel like a different person.

3. Drama therapy also acts as a sort of group therapy – there is a group that needs to successfully work together in order to put on a show, which requires mutual cooperation and effective communication.

Questions to Guide the Reader

1. What is drama therapy?

2. How can playing a part on stage help a patient delve into their own trauma?

3. Why does Van der Kolk believe that ancient Greek dramas were used as reenactments for traumatized Greek soldiers?

Action Plan: Part Five

1. Part Five offers many different sources of potential treatment: yoga, mindfulness, CBT, EMDR, drama therapy, and animal therapy. If you are struggling, don't be afraid to get creative.

2. Ask your mental health professional for more information on one or several of these therapies.

3. Do not hesitate to seriously consider it a viable treatment opportunity if a professional offers an "experimental" type of therapy, such as drama therapy, creative writing, horse riding lessons, yoga, or anything they believe could help a patient reconnect with themselves.

Epilogue

Summary

In his conclusion, Van der Kolk notes that society as a whole is becoming more aware of – and having more frank discussions about – mental health and trauma. As research increases and new techniques are adopted, overall treatment of traumatized people trends slowly for the better. However, there are also numerous continued societal failures, such as a disproportionate incarceration rate for trauma victims. Van der Kolk states that modern pharmacology and psychiatry have compounded these issues.

Van der Kolk goes on to say that medical providers and the general public alike must focus on children – both in preventing childhood trauma and in providing better support systems for traumatized children. He further states that this will require more support for struggling families and schools, as young trauma survivors must be provided space to learn and practice healthy coping strategies.

Dr. Van der Kolk concludes that trauma is America's most urgent public health issue and places the onus on readers to act on the knowledge they have been provided.

Conclusion

Dr. Bessel van der Kolk's lifetime of work with trauma patients has been a labor of love. In *The Body Keeps the Score,* Kolk leaves no stone unturned, exploring trauma healing techniques from ancient medicine to the latest in cutting-age research. In describing his own journey navigating the medical field, it's clear that Van der Kolk has always been deeply sensitive to the needs of those who have experienced trauma.

Throughout the book, Van der Kolk's main theme is that, in order for patients to recover from a traumatic experience, they need to be able to reconnect with themselves. If they cannot do this, as the title of this book suggests, their body will "keep a tally" of their traumas. Unchecked trauma can – and does — cause a variety of physical ailments; Van der Kolk found that the majority of his trauma patients also had some sort of autoimmune disease.

The author continues to explore the differences between trauma patients and mental health patients who present symptoms without debilitating trauma at its source. He finds that childhood trauma rewires the brains of adolescents; violence at the hands of loved ones causes physical problems, ranging from memory failure to self-mutilation. Everywhere Van der Kolk looked, there was a patient who needed help, and had not yet gotten anywhere in therapy.

Utilizing his expertise in service of those who need it the most, *The Body Keeps the Score* speaks equally effectively to readers, researchers, and caregivers. The book provides a thorough understanding of the context, history, and treatment of all types of traumatic experiences.

Background Information About *The Body Keeps the Score*

Trauma can adversely affect its survivors' capacities for pleasure, socialization, self-control, and trust. From sports to drama to yoga, *The Body Keeps the Score* draws from decades of Dr. Bessel van der Kolk's own research about the effects of trauma on the human body. Using the latest scientific research and consensus, Van der Kolk demonstrates how trauma literally reshapes our brains.

He offers simple, actionable steps for combating the physical and mental damage caused by trauma, as well as explores cutting-edge treatments.

The book has been well received by peers, readers, and critics alike, having obtained endorsements from leading researchers in the field. As of 2021, the book has spent more than 141 weeks on the *New York Times* bestseller list for nonfiction.

Background Information About Dr. Bessel van der Kolk

Dr. Bessel van der Kolk, born in 1943, is a psychiatrist, researcher, and educator. He is presently a professor of Psychiatry at the Boston University School of Medicine. He is located in Boston, MA, where he has spent most of his training, education, and career. His specialty is PTSD and, of course, this book has made him famous for being notable as such. He is the founder and former medical director of the Trauma Center at the Justice Resource Institute or JRI, also in Massachusetts, and a cofounder of the National Child Traumatic Stress Network.

He has spent decades working with trauma survivors, from combat veterans to sexual abuse victims and others. His forward thinking has made a generation of psychiatrists change the way they view and treat their trauma patients.

He has a website, www.besselvanderkolk.com, which provides a free newsletter and educates the public about his work and his study in the medical field of PTSD.

Details On Treatment Options

During the course of this book, Dr. Van der Kolk describes several treatments that are commonly used for, or may be useful to, trauma survivors. In some cases, treatments mentioned by the author are actively recommended to patients. These methods are described in further detail here:

Cognitive Behavioral Therapy (CBT)

Cognitive behavioral therapy is a form of mental health care that aims to treat mental illnesses through traditional "talk therapy," in which psychotherapists communicate verbally with patients to work through symptoms associated with depression, anxiety, and other disorders. Though CBT has been shown to be effective when combined with other forms of treatment, such as hypnotherapy, and especially for insomnia and anxiety, talk therapy alone is rarely enough to heal trauma.

- *Try it yourself:* CBT must be done with an experienced, licensed psychotherapist. Most forms of health insurance cover all or most of the cost of talk therapy. For more information, ask a health care practitioner for a referral to someone near you.

Eye Movement Desensitization and Reprocessing (EMDR)

Eye Movement Desensitization and Reprocessing or EMDR is a form of psychotherapy in which the patient is intentionally asked to recall distressing images, at which point the treatment provider redirects the patient's eye focus via some form of bilateral stimulation. This method of treatment is still relatively new and continues to be researched by professionals in the field, but has been shown to be effective in areas such as treating combat-induced PTSD.

- *Try it yourself:* Like CBT, EMDT must be practiced with an experienced psychotherapist. Practitioners can be found online on free databases such as ZocDoc.

Yoga

Yoga is a form of physical and mental exercise originating in India, which emphasizes "quieting" the mind and practicing stillness. In *The Body Keeps the Score*, Dr. Van der Kolk says about yoga, "It's about becoming safe to feel what you feel…. Neuroscience research shows that the only way we can change the way we feel is by becoming aware of our inner experience and learning to befriend what is going on inside ourselves." Gentle physical practices that cultivate a feeling of safety in the body can be far more effective than cognitive work alone. By slowly and safely building a gentle practice where you are in control of the boundaries, how far and how long you go at every moment can be transformational in your healing.

- *Try it yourself:* Various guides to "beginner" yoga are available for free online, including via YouTube, the *New York Times*, and *Self* magazine online.

Meditation

Meditation is a form of mindfulness that is designed to focus on our thoughts and energy, usually with the end result of achieving calm and stability. In the text, Dr. Van der Kolk states that meditation and other forms of mindfulness are particularly effective when combined with physical practices, such as yoga.

- *Try it yourself:* A common form of meditation begins with closing your eyes and focusing solely on your breathing. If you find it difficult to keep your mind from wandering, instrumental music may help. Meditation guides can also be found for free online, including from YouTube, the *New York Times,* and *Wikihow.*

Discussion Questions

Use these questions to deepen your understanding of this book and get the most out of its contents.

1. According to *The Body Keeps the Score*, what are some possible reasons for today's prevalence of mental illness?
2. Based on *The Body Keeps the Score,* how does it seem most trauma survivors are treated?
3. What do you suppose is Dr. Van der Kolk's reason for including his real patients in the book?
4. Dr. Van der Kolk notes several differences between trauma that affects children and trauma that affects adults. What are some of those differences? Are they similar in any way?
5. What large-scale social changes would provide better support for people who have experienced trauma?
6. Many people find their mental health treatment to be ineffective. What reasons does the book suggest may be the cause of this?
7. Dr. Van der Kolk mentions the influence of several other researchers and educators. Which two would you say most impacted his views? Why?
8. What are some physical changes that take place in the brain as a result of trauma?
9. Could substituting in-person communication with electronic or virtual communication contribute to trauma? Why?
10. Of the treatments suggested in Part 5, which are "top-down," and which are "bottom-up?" How can you tell?

11. How and why do patients need to reconnect their bodies with their minds?
12. How can yoga and meditation work as part of a treatment plan, along with CBT, versus just the CBT?
13. What is EMDR and how does it work?
14. What is the DSM and how many times has it been updated? How has it been received by the public? How is it perceived by doctors?

More books from Smart Reads

Summary of Breath: The New Science of a Lost Art By
James Nestor
Workbook for What Happened to You? By Oprah Winfrey
and Dr. Bruce Perry
Workbook for Atomic Habits By James Clear

Thank You

Hope you've enjoyed your reading experience.

We here at Smart Reads will always strive to deliver to you the highest quality guides.

So I'd like to thank you for supporting us and reading until the very end.

Before you go, would you mind leaving us a review on Amazon?

It will mean a lot to us and support us creating high quality guides for you in the future.

Thanks once again!

Warmly yours,

The Smart Reads Team

Download Your Free Gift

As a way to say "Thank You" for being a fan of our series,
I've included a free gift for you:

Brain Health: How to Nurture and Nourish Your Brain For
Top Performance

Go to www.smart-reads.com to get your
FREE book.

The Smart Reads Team

Made in the USA
Las Vegas, NV
08 March 2022